# THE SEA IN SHIPS

# THE SEA
# IN SHIPS

## THE STORY OF
## A SAILING SHIP'S VOYAGE
## ROUND CAPE HORN

BY
## ALAN J. VILLIERS

AUTHOR OF "FALMOUTH FOR ORDERS", "BY WAY OF CAPE HORN",
"VANISHED FLEETS", ETC.

With 112 photographs by the author

LONDON
GEORGE ROUTLEDGE AND SONS LTD.
Broadway House: 68-74 Carter Lane, E.C.
1932

Rolling Home to dear old England,
Rolling Home across the sea,
Rolling Home to dear old England,
Rolling Home, Fair Land, to thee.
*(From an old sailing ship shanty)*

# FOREWORD

I am not a photographer. Technical excellence is not claimed for any of these photographs. Beyond the commonplace manipulation of the ordinary cheap Kodak, I know nothing of photography. All that I have done has been to take film and camera to sea, insert the film in the camera, and work the shutter in the approved manner when appropriate subjects presented themselves.

I could not develop the resultant negatives as there was insufficient fresh water available. In any case I did not know how to develop, simple as the process is. I put the rolls of film away and kept them until I came into port.

With the exception of two or three excellent photographs which have been supplied by my friend Captain F. C. Poyser, of the Nautical Photo Agency, these pictures were all taken in the course of two voyages—one in the Finnish four-masted barque Herzogin Cecilie, from Port Lincoln to Falmouth for orders in 1928, and the other with my friend Ronald Walker in the Finnish full-rigged ship Grace Harwar from Wallaroo to Queenstown for orders in 1929. Ronald Walker was a real photographer: he was killed early in the voyage. Some of these photographs have already appeared in my books "Falmouth for Orders" and "By Way of Cape Horn," and for the right to reproduce these I am indebted to the publisher, Mr. Geoffrey Bles.

If there is any excellence in these pictures, the credit is due to the foolproof qualities of the modern cheap camera and not to the skill of the photographer.

LONDON,
   *October* 18, 1931.

A. J. VILLIERS.

# THE SEA IN SHIPS

THERE are still—October, 1931—about thirty big deep-sea square-rigged sailing ships in commission in general trade. There are about ten others in commission purely as training-ships, but these do not go round Cape Horn and with them I am not concerned. The thirty are almost exclusively Germans and Finns. There are also three Swedes and one American. Twenty are Finnish; five are Germans. The Germans are the very fine four-masted barques of the Hamburg Laeisz Line—Passat, Palma, Priwall, Peking, and Padua—which are engaged in the carriage of nitrates from Chile to European ports. They go out to Chile round the Horn, and sail Home round the Horn again—twice round Cape Horn each voyage, often three times round, and even four, in one year.

The Finns and the Swedes are in the grain trade from Australia. The carriage of heavy grain, in sacks, from small South Australian ports to the United Kingdom is practically the only trade left to the big sailing ships. They make one voyage annually, sailing from Europe in ballast to Australia in September and October, loading their wheat in small ports where prompt delivery and quick turn-round are not to be expected, and sailing Home again from Australia in the early months of the year. They usually take about three months to sail to Australia in ballast, and four months to come Home with the wheat. Two months are spent in port, so that a round voyage occupies about nine months. For the other three months of the year, not having anything else to do, they are laid up, usually in their little home port of Mariehamn, in the Aland Islands.

The sailing ships are able to take a share in the carriage of Australian grain to England, even during the most depressed periods of shipping history, because they are run in a most economical manner, because they do not care how long they take to load, and because it does not matter how long the wheat takes to make the voyage Home. As well as carrying the wheat, the sailing ship gives it free warehousing for four or five months. During this time there is a gambler's chance that the market may have improved.

Then, too, the sailing ship can afford to accept a lower rate of freight than the steamer and still show a profit. She is satisfied with a lower rate of profit than the steamer. Because time is of little account and because her day-to-day running costs are very low (under the Finnish flag), she can afford to accept cargoes from slow-loading, out-of-the-way ports which would be ruinous to the steamers. The steamers would carry all the Australian grain, if they could. There are enough of them hunting for cargoes. They have already robbed the sailing ship of everything else— even Peruvian guano. Sentiment does not get the Cape Horn ships their cargoes. It is a plain business proposition. Where, for example, a big steamer could accept a grain charter to load at Port Adelaide for 32 shillings a ton and know that there would be a small margin of profit because the grain could be quickly loaded there, she would have to refuse such a charter for a small port where she would be dependent upon irregular deliveries of the wheat spread over a month. The day-to-day charges during that month would more than absorb the small profit.

But the total running costs of a Finnish Cape Horn sailing ship do not exceed £400 a month—counting stores, wages, canvas, everything. The crews are paid very little, able seamen's wages being less than £2 a month and even second mates being fortunate to receive £4 10s. Masters receive about £12 monthly. The ships are not insured, and there is almost no depreciation on them. They were all bought second-hand, at prices not greatly exceeding their scrap-iron values. Many of the crews are young boys of different nationalities who pay the owner for the right to work in his ships. They are called apprentices, and pay about £40 for three years' indentures. They receive about £1 a month as wages and get a very thorough training, for the simple reason that, since there aren't any other sailors in the ships, they very quickly have to learn to do all the sailoring themselves. This is a rough school but a very efficient one, and the boys rapidly develop into first-class sailors. Many of them qualify as able seamen after one round voyage, and as second mates after three years.

To conclude this dissertation upon the economic side of the modern square-rigged ships, a few figures as to the actual running costs and charges on a round voyage in one of these ships will convey a clear idea of how it is they survive. We shall take the famous sailing ship Herzogin Cecilie as an excellent example. She was bought by Captain Gustaf Erikson, of Mariehamn, just after the war, for £4,250. She was a German training ship originally, and had been handed over to the French as part of the reparations payments. The French, not having any use for her at the time —they had many square-rigged ships of their own—sold her for what she would fetch. Her real value was about £20,000; if she had changed hands in the war she would have brought £60,000. Captain Erikson, then, got her very cheaply. She has paid for herself *four times over* during the ten years she has been under his control.

She was chartered the other day to load grain in South Australia for the United Kingdom at 31 shillings a ton. She loads about 4,800 tons; therefore, her cheque for carrying that grain to England will be £7,440. Her total expenses for the entire voyage—out and Home—should not exceed £6,000 at the extreme limit. Therefore she should show a profit of at least £1,440 on the voyage. For that £7,440, she has to sail to Australia in ballast, discharge the ballast, load the grain, sail Home again, discharge the grain, load more ballast, and go back to Mariehamn to lay up. The crew have to be paid, new sails have to be bought; pilotage, port charges, tugs, butchers, bakers, paint merchants, agents, brokers, stevedores, wharf labourers—all these must be paid out of that £7,440. Dry docking must be paid for; fresh water must be bought. Office charges have to be met. (These are small as the owner is his own office.) The list looks frightening, but it is not, really. I should like to have the change from £6,000 when I had paid for that voyage.

It costs only about 1s. 3d. a day to feed a sailor, and sailors eat a lot. The entire wage bill of the ship would not exceed £100 a month. For nine months, then, that charge would be £900. Food and stores and canvas and so on would cost, for the round voyage, about £1,000, including dry-docking in Europe before setting out. If there are no repairs necessary, this is not expensive. The total costs in Australia, covering port dues, pilotage, loading, and everything else, would not exceed £2,200. Australian currency, in which this amount is paid, is 30 per cent below sterling, in which the freight is received. The owner's real expense for this section of the voyage, then, is £1,540 and not £2,200 (provided Australian currency remains in the same relation to sterling, of course). The total costs on the European side, including towage, pilotage, discharging, and the run in ballast to Mariehamn, should not exceed £2,500.

Therefore we have a rough balance-sheet as follows:—

| Debit | £ | Credit | £ |
|---|---|---|---|
| Crew costs .. .. .. | 900 | Freight .. .. | 7,440 |
| Stores, canvas, etc. .. .. | 1,000 | | |
| Australian costs .. .. | 1,540 | | |
| European costs .. .. | 2,500 | | |
| Total | 5,940 | Total | 7,440 |
| | | *Profit* | 1,500 |

Of course, to make this profit, it is important that no accidents should occur and that there should be no undue delays. It is not as easy as it may sound; otherwise there would be more sailing-ship owners. It takes courage and enterprise to run these ships, and the favourable circumstances of the high Australian exchange might end at any time. There are good years, but there are also bad. Captain Erikson's ships give him plenty of trouble. There are fifteen of them in the Cape Horn trade; each year at least two are in more or less serious trouble. This year there is a salvage claim against the Pommern, and the Ponape was in serious collision. The Killoran and the Pommern both lost lives coming round the Horn. The Olivebank and the Hougomont made very long voyages and small profits—if any. The Killoran had to be re-classed, at considerable expense.

Now they are all sailing out to Australia once again, and sixteen of them have been chartered at good rates. These are the four-masted barques Herzogin Cecilie, Lawhill, Melbourne, Pommern, Ponape, Parma, Archibald Russell, Abraham Rydberg, C. B. Pedersen, Olivebank, and Viking (all but two of which are Captain Erikson's); the barques Favell, Killoran, Penang, and Winterhude; and the four-masted barquentine Mozart. The Abraham Rydberg and the C. B. Pedersen fly the Swedish flag; the rest are Finns. Of the sixteen ships, twelve are Captain Erikson's. None is British.

The ships sail out round the Cape of Good Hope and Home again by way of the Horn—that grand old road that hundreds of splendid British ships have sailed, but which now they sail no more. They go direct. They put in at no ports, and make no deviations. They carry no wireless. They have no fripperies, no luxuries. They go quietly about their business, which is the carriage of grain, and bother with nothing else. You will not see them from passing steamers, except sometimes off the chops of the Channel, or in the North-East Trades where the Rio Lane crosses the Homeward Bounders' track, or off the Azores in a calm. Thirty sailing ships are not many, spread over the world's oceans. The chance to see one at sea is becoming increasingly rarer.

If they sail from Mariehamn, as most do, they take their stores aboard off Kopenhagen and stand out into the Atlantic by way of the north of Scotland. They give the English Channel a wide berth, if they can. Once around the British Isles, they make their way as best they can to the North-East Trades and so to the Line, and thence through the South-East Trades "full and by" and to the southern Horse Latitudes and the Roaring Forties. In Forty South they turn eastwards and run fleetly for Australia before the strong westerly gales of those high latitudes, nor do they incline one degree towards the north until their longitude has been run down and they have come almost to their landfall. This is usually wild Cape Borda, on Kangaroo Island, at the entrance to Spencer Gulf in South Australia, and this is the first land they will have seen since leaving Denmark. It is not at all uncommon to make the land less than 80 days out from Europe. I myself have made it in 70 days, in the four-masted barque Lawhill from Bordeaux. We were 74 days from port to port, and only 70 days from departure to landfall. The German ship Grief (now broken up) sailed out from Valencia in 69 days. The Lawhill made three consecutive voyages in 78, 74, and 70 days. She is not a fast ship. The Hougomont and the Ponape sailed out together in 82 days, and the Favell in 86. The average is about 95 days. All these times have been made since the war.

It takes anything from six weeks to two months to load the wheat, principally because the ballast is discharged by the crew into the sea and, to do this, the ship has to be sailed from the wharf to some deep spot called the "ballast grounds," where for days and days the boys have to buckle down to it like navvies and shift a thousand tons of stone and sand. This done (a stiffening of wheat has been loaded at the wharf first), the ship sails back to her berth again and full loading proceeds. Tugs are not used. There are none at these small ports, although, if necessary, one could be brought from Port Adelaide, a night's steam away. This would be done only in cases of great danger.

With the grain aboard and the hatches battened down, all the gear rigged and the ship ready for sea, at last the great day comes when the pilot comes aboard and the ship is off. They sail right from the very wharf, although they usually warp out to an anchorage first and get under way from there. In some of the ports the waters are restricted and narrow, but there is no thought of engaging a tow-boat from Port Adelaide. The ship takes herself to sea, and God's wind blows her to England.

What a long time it seems to be at sea, and how far off seems England! Tramping round the fo'c'sle head getting the anchor up at Port Lincoln, the hard 16,000-mile road stretches out interminably before you. You feel that the wind can never blow you all that way. Weeks and weeks of incessant work, the long, weary run to Cape Horn—6,000 miles—battling past the Falkland Islands and through the southern Horse Latitudes, fishing for the South-East Trades, sweltering on the Line, wandering through the North-East Trades making too much westing and ending up, as like as not, in the weed on the outskirts of the Sargasso Sea (there is nothing there except crabs), and then meandering slowly through the northern Horse Latitudes, becalmed off the Azores, the last—the very last—long lap from the Azores to the Channel with fresh wind and driving spume, and then, at the voyage end, head wind in the chops of the Channel—head wind or fog and calm. 'Twas ever thus; it is a hard road.

But it is an interesting one. It is a man's life. It has very great compensations. It is one of the few unspoilt walks of life which still remain. There are no artificialities about it. There are no newspapers, no stock exchanges, no politicians. It is extraordinary how one may make a long voyage in a sailing ship, through calm and storm, under blue skies and grey, in rain and in sunshine. There are passing clouds, but on the whole all is well with the world. There are no crises. There are no "grave political events." There are no stock exchange slumps, or bank failures; no rumblings of war.

And yet, when you come into the first port and the pilot brings aboard a newspaper, you find that half the world is mad and the other half dangerously sick; that there are grave possibilities of at least two wars; that the politicians of all countries have made a terrible mess of things, and that there have been at least eighteen murders in the preceding week. One throws the newspaper down in disgust and longs for the freshness of the sea outside and the beauty of the swelling sails.

The run to Cape Horn is the worst part of the voyage, and that, very properly, is over first. The first week at sea is rather long, after the softness of port. The watch and watch system is hard for a few days, with its broken sleep and its many awakenings upon the same day. Ashore, when you awaken from a sleep, it is another day. At sea, you may awaken three times on the same day, and yet not have had sufficient sleep. In the early stages this circumstance makes the days drag and the time appear long.

Very soon after leaving Australia—as soon as possible—the ship dips down into the West Winds and turns her head eastwards for Cape Horn. She goes down to 45 South, 48, 50, but she does not usually stand right down to the cold latitudes of the Horn until she is close up with that wild Headland. Cape Horn is in 57 South; it is usual to go down there only for the rounding. The gales shriek and the rain squalls fly by incessantly; the heavy seas sweep constantly over the hard-pressed decks, and the ship, down to shortened canvas, runs on gleaming wet from deck to truck in full storm. The giant seas rush majestically past, each depositing something of itself aboard as it swings by, seemingly intent upon the ship's destruction yet never succeeding. Here the untamed albatross floats upon the air and laughs at the hurricane; sometimes one is treated to the glorious sight of a bull blue whale cavorting himself pompously in the crest of a huge wave.

The hail lashes and the wind roars; the rain and the sea combine to make the ship a wet misery; the gallery fire is out, the fo'c'sle all but under water; it is hell to hold her at the wheel. Yet there is a wild fascination about it all: let her run! She is game. Beautiful old ship, she has run here many a time and beaten all the gales. She can do it again. She does!

It seems an awful lot of trouble to go to, sometimes (if one ever reflects upon it), just to bring 4,000 tons of wheat to England. Who cares about the wheat, once it is delivered? Who cares about the ship, when the voyage is done? And yet it is a game endeavour.

For anything from six weeks to two-and-a-half months you are wet through and cold. You do not get enough sleep. The crews are small; all hands make only one good watch, these days. Sometimes, when you most need warm food, there is none because the sea has swamped the galley fire. There is no steam heat. There is no drying-room for your clothes. You get wet and you stay wet; there isn't anything else to do. You wrap burlap about your feet, and lash your oilskins at wrist and ankle with stout ropeyarns. You might just as well not bother. Burlap will not keep you warm; no oilskins made can keep you dry for long. If the rain water does not beat them, the sea does . . . . Watch after watch, day after day, week after week, rain and hail and cold, storm and gale and hurricane: what a life!

But the sea is not all Cape Horn, all ocean not the Cape Horn road.

There comes a day when the Horn is passed, when the voyage seems half over though but the first landmark is gone. Before Cape Horn, no one speaks of England. In a dull kind of way, you know that you are bound to Falmouth or to Queenstown. But first you must get around Cape Horn. The voyage splits itself naturally into three main sections—departure to the Horn; the Horn to the Line; and from the Line, Home. As each is begun, you look forward only to its accomplishment and do not think of the others. You do not speak of Home until the Line is passed and the Doldrums have been negotiated. Here, I think, lies the secret why the four-month period does not seem so long. There is no monotony about it. There is far too much of interest, and there is far too much work.

After the Horn, we stand up inside the Falklands, off the coast of

Patagonia, to take advantage of a favouring current before standing over in a north-easterly direction to get through the Horse Latitudes and grope for the Trades. In the Horse Latitudes the good Cape Horn sails come down and the Tropic rags go aloft in their stead. Sail is changed twice a voyage—the whole suit. The best sails are bent only in the worst weather; for Trade winds and Doldrum calm, anything that will hold the wind will do.

Now the flying fish come, and the barefoot days. It is pleasant to scrub the decks down every morning and evening, and to swim over the side in patches of calm, to fish for albacore from the bowsprit-end or dolphins from the poop. For day after day the Trade blows true and the sun shines. A pull on brace and halliards in the mornings, and all is plain sailing for the day; no calls for all hands, or even for the watch by night, no hard squalls, no shortening down, no troubles! This is making up for the bitterness of the Horn; this is good. Yet too much of it would pall.

You do not get too much of it. The fresher the Trades, the sooner you are through them; the better they blow the sooner do they bring you to the Line and Doldrum calm. There you must sweat and toil, with infinite pains for infinitesimal gain; hauling round the yards for every catspaw, with the sun directly overhead and the pitch bubbling up in the deck seams and no spare fresh water to drink. If you are lucky, you will be out of this in four days; if you are unlucky, it may be three weeks.

The Doldrums is the worst part of the voyage; calm and baffling light winds are worse than storms. You can do something about a storm. The calm beats you.

It is a relief to everybody when the North-East Trade comes. The skipper's temper is at its worst in the Doldrums; his mood affects everyone. If he growls at the mates and is like a pig with a sore head, they snarl at the sailors in the watch on deck, and fret in watch below. The sailors snarl at each other, and even the ship's pig longs for the cook's knife and an end to his misery.

But what a difference the coming of the Trades makes! Everybody smiles then, and the Old Man puts on a collar and shaves off his beard. The mate, taking the cue, jokes with the boy at the wheel, and the sail-maker sings while he wields his palm and needle. The steward forgets that there are no more prunes for the sweet soup; nobody minds that the lime juice is all used up or that the salt horse is saltier and horsier than ever. On the lookout by night you think of Paradise in terms of juicy steaks; at the wheel you ponder on an after-life of roast beef and Yorkshire pudding, where the water is not rust-stained and cement-tainted and there is a little to spare for a bath.

A fortnight of good Trades brings you to the Horse Latitudes of the north—that belt of unsteady breezes that lies between the Trades and the west winds further north. Here you must make what way you can; it is better than the Doldrums. The wisps of wind are not so deceptive; any may develop into a good steady breeze. You may lie a while in calm near the Azores, if you are unlucky enough to have got too close to those islands. But then you are within striking distance of Home and the voyage-end, fresh steaks and all night in! From the Azores to the Channel you may be six days or sixteen; it depends on the wind. All the voyage depends on that. It usually follows, if you have had a bad run to the Horn, you have a good passage through the Atlantic; if a good run to the Horn, then a bad passage on the next sections. The voyage balances out; a calm here offsets a storm there, just as a lost watch below one day is offset by a farmer in the Trades. (A farmer's watch is a watch when you haven't a wheel turn or lookout and the mate doesn't find anything for you to do. It does not occur often.)

With maddening frequency, the last few days before the anchor is down in Queenstown or Falmouth Bay are the worst of the voyage. Shore clothes have been taken out and aired; land birds are seen; the blue water shoals into green; the smoke of steamers blurs the horizon. Yet head wind may delay you for weeks, almost within sight of your destination; or fog blot everything out just as you reach soundings. You have to grin and bear it. You have to put up with what you get and do the best you can about it. That is the whole basis of sailing-ship life. The ship spreads her sails to God's wind, and her people have to sail her Home. She takes what the wind and the sea have to offer her and makes the best of them; nor does she ask for anything more. Not for her the honk of engines or reek of smoke! She sails on serene in her own loveliness, blending perfectly with her surroundings. A curious blend of science and beauty developed through the centuries, she still finds work to do, and will, I think, while the wind blows.

And so we come to landfall and anchor-down and voyage end. We may have given a life for Cape Horn; we may have lost someone overboard. We may have been hungry, grossly overworked and badly underpaid. We may have been face to face with death upon occasion.

Yet it was all a grand adventure, very much worth while.

I. WAITING FOR HER CARGO

2. THE GOLDEN GRAIN COMES ABOARD

3. DEEP LADEN—READY FOR THE LONG VOYAGE

4.   **GETTING** UNDER WEIGH

5.  HEAVE-HO, MY HEARTIES!   SETTING THE SAIL

6.  ALL SAIL SET AND DRAWING: LOOKING UP THE MAIN MAST

7.   FREE OF THE LAND: THE VOYAGE BEGINS

8. FAIR WIND AND FLOWING SAILS!

9.  GOING STRONG: LOOKING DIRECTLY DOWN ON THE BOWS

10.  THE GLISTENING WAKE: LOOKING FROM THE MIZZEN TOP DIRECTLY DOWN

11. BREEZING A LITTLE: WE MAKE FAST THE ROYALS

12. TWO HANDS TO THE MAIN ROYAL

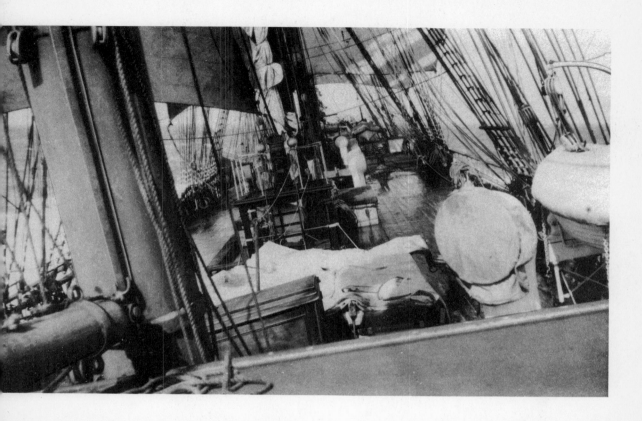

13.   A DECK VIEW—SOUTH OF TASMANIA

14.　DOING TWELVE!　(FROM THE BOWSPRIT END —"HERZOGIN CECILIE")

15. THIS IS THE LIFE

16.  WIND AFT: WE BEGIN THE LONG RUN TO CAPE HORN

17.   SQUARE YARDS, COURSES FAST, AND BOILING WAKE

18. RUNNING FOURTEEN KNOTS IN A FRESHENING GALE: LOOKING AFT FROM THE FORE-TOP

19.  A LITTLE WATER BEGINS TO SLOP ABOARD

20.   MAKING FAST THE MIZZEN T'GALL'NTS'L

21.   A LITTLE WATER BEGINS TO SLOP ABOARD

22.   WET DECKS AND RUNNING HEAVILY: THE WATCH CLEWING UP A SAIL ON THE
FOREMAST

23. ALOFT AND FURL IT!

24.  THE FLY-LIKE FIGURES OF THE HANDS ALOFT

24A.  150 FEET ABOVE THE BOILING SEA: WORKING ON A T'GALLN'T YARD

25.   ALL HANDS MAKE THE MAINS'L FAST

26. THE STORMY ALBATROSS
HOVERS ALOFT

*(Photo: Nautical Photo Agency)*

27. SCUPPERS FULL:
A HEAVY SEA

28.   THE SEA SWEEPS UNCHECKED ABOARD

29.   AN UGLY BREAKING SEA RUSHES AT THE SHIP

30. SMOTHERED IN SEA AND SPRAY: A CAPE HORN DECK VIEW

31.   FOR SIX WEEKS THE DECKS WERE LIKE THIS

32.   FROM THE CROJACK YARD

33.   WET WORK IN THE WAIS[
THERE IS ALWAYS WOR[

34.   STILL WIND AND SEA INCREASE: FULL STORM
(*Photo: Nautical Photo Agency*)

35    BLOWING A HURRICANE: ONE OF THE MOST THRILLING PICTURES BROUGHT FROM CAPE HORN
*(Photo: Nautical Photo Agency)*

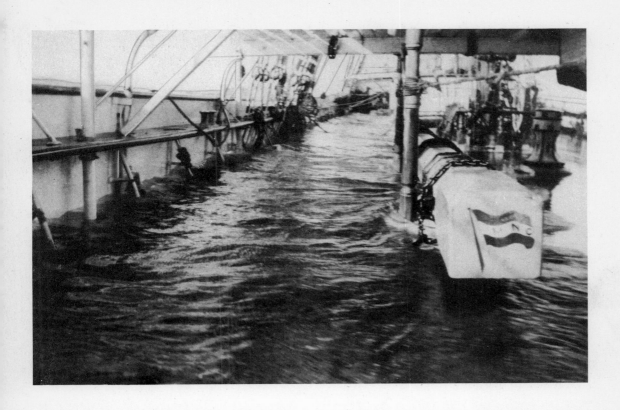

36. NEXT MORNING: THE BREEZE GONE DOWN, BUT MAIN DECK HEAVILY AWASH
*(Photo: Nautical Photo Agency)*

37.  NOOSING THE MIZZEN LOWER TOPS'L, AFTER THE STORM

38.    TRAMPING ROUND THE CAPSTAN, STRETCHING A TOPS'L

39.   RONALD GREGORY WALKER, SACRIFICED TO
THE STORM

40.   THE BURIAL SERVICE, MAY 26TH, 1929

41.   FLAG HALF-MAST: THE SHIP RUNS ON

42.   PEACEFUL EVENING, 55° SOUTH

43. LEAKING! MANNING THE PUMPS

44.   THE FIGUREHEAD KEEPS GUARD (A BOBSTAY PHOTOGRAPH)

45. THE ALBATROSSES COME ABOARD IN A CALM

46. JUST LIKE A BIG GOOSE

47.   AROUND THE HORN: STANDING UP PAST THE FALKLAND ISLANDS

48. FAREWELL CAPE HORN! THE OLD SEA-DOGS ARE PLEASED

49.  A GOOD BREEZE IN THE SOUTH ATLANTIC: FROM THE WEATHER
FORE YARDARM

50.   BETTER WEATHER NOW: SUNSHINE AND SHADE

51.  SLOW AHEAD: A GENTLE BREEZE

52.   THE MORNING JOB: OVERHAULING BUNTLINES

53. STRIPPED TO THE WAIST: AT WORK HIGH IN THE
RIGGING

54. OVER THE CROSS-TREES (IN TRADE WIND GARB)

55.  A TICKLISH JOB

56. TIME TO CHANGE SAIL

57.   A RECALCITRANT BUNTLINE

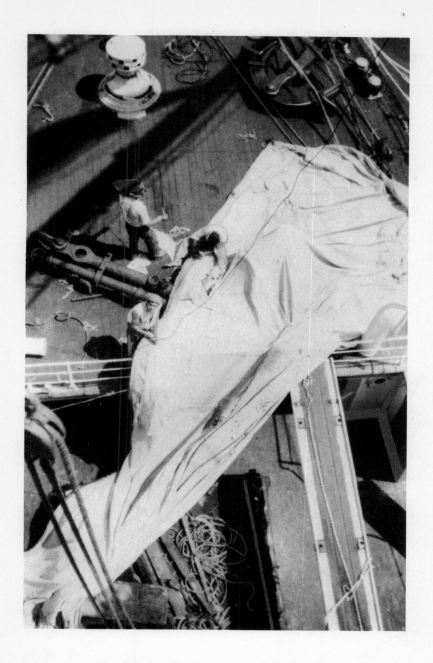

58. BENDING THE TRADE WIND FORES'L TO ITS GEAR

59.  CHANGING THE MAINS'L

60    HAULING HOME A LIGHT WIND GALL'NTS'L

61.   A SAILOR'S IDEA OF A "GOOD" JOB: BENDING A ROYAL ("HERZOGIN CECILIE")

62.   THIS WEATHER BRINGS THE SKIPPER'S FOWLS ON DECK

63. DOG WATCH RECREATION: LEARNING TO SPLICE

64.   AT THE MAIN TRUCK

65. SUNDAY'S JOB (WHEN THERE IS ANY RAIN-WATER TO BE HAD)

66.   SUNDAY AFTERNOON: CLEAN SHIRT, CLEAN SHIP, CLEAN LIFE, CLEAN SEA

67.   RAMBLING THROUGH THE S.E. TRADE: THE CUTWATER, PHOTO
GRAPHED FROM A LINE SLUNG FROM THE BOWSPRIT-END

68. SAILORS' WORK IS NEVER DONE: MENDING SAILS

69.   CAPTAIN DE CLOUX SHOOTS THE SUN

70.   A TROPIC SQUALL: OUR MAIN TOPS'L SPLITS A SEAM AND HAS TO COME IN

71.   A BIRD'S-EYE VIEW OF THE BOYS ON THE TOPS'L YARD

72.   ALOFT ON A TROPIC DAY, WITH SUN ON THE SEA FAR BELOW

73. OUR STOWAWAY FINDS A JOB ON DECK IN THE GOOD WEATHER

74.   WE HOVE TO ONE DAY,—

75.   PUT A BOAT OUT,—

76.   AND TOOK A PHOTOGRAPH

77. BLOW, BLOW, GOOD WIND!

78.    RUNNING FAST UP TO THE LINE

79.   STOPPED: THE SAILS HANG LIFELESS IN DOLDRUM CALM

80.  STAGNATION: LOOKING UP THE MAINMAST IN FLAT CALM

81.   BACKING AND FILLING BEAUTIFULLY BUT NOT GETTING ANYWHERE

82. THE SKIPPER, TIRED OF WHISTLING FOR A WIND, GOES AFTER THE
FISH

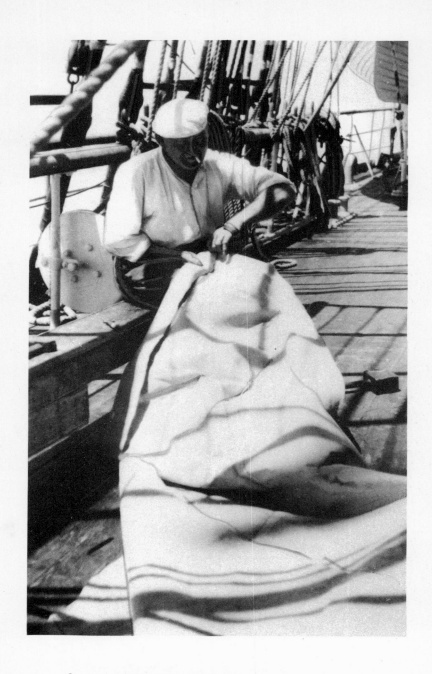

83.   OR SEWS SAIL IN THE SUN

84.   A DOLDRUMS BATH: THIS IS THE LIFE!

85. WE OVERHAUL ANOTHER SHIP

86.   WE PASS THE "C. B. PEDERSEN," SAILING BY HIS WEATHER SIDE

87.   RIGHT ROUND HIM: NOW HE IS A-LEE

88.   NOW WE LEAVE HIM ASTERN

89.   KING NEPTUNE COMES ABOARD, WITH HIS WIFE

90.   CAPTAIN SVENSSON WITH MRS. NEPTUNE AND THE DEAN OF THE EQUATORIAL
CATHEDRAL

91.   THE CHIEF INQUISITORS—DOCTOR AND NURSE

92.   THE COURT ON THE MAIN DECK ("GRACE HARWAR")

93. HOLDING HER BOWSPRIT AHEAD TO CATCH THE BREEZE: WE PICK
UP THE N.E. TRADES

94.    A FRESHENING TRADE: LOOKING DOWN FROM THE MIZZEN TRUCK

95.   CHURNING UP THE SEA: SHE PUTS HER NOSE ALMOST UNDER WATER

96.    A PATCH OF CALM AGAIN, NEAR THE AZORES

97.   WE CHANGE SAIL AGAIN, FOR THE LAST LAP

98.   RE-BENDING A GOOD ROYAL

99. ROLLING UP THE TROPIC SAILS

100.   ON THE LAST LAP: THE NORTH ATLANTIC BREEZE BLOWS OUT A SAIL

101.  CARRYING THE GOOD SHIP HOME

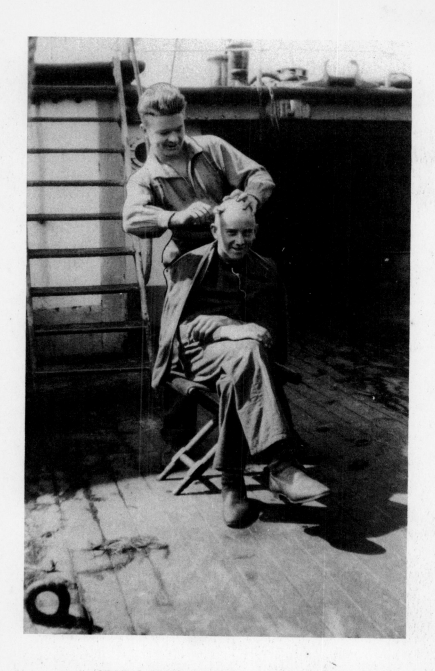

102.  GETTING READY FOR PORT, AND ALL IT MEANS

103.   A LONG PULL AND A STRONG PULL

104.   SAILORS ON THE "GRACE HARWAR"

105. SHACKLING ON THE CABLES OFF THE CHOPS OF THE CHANNEL

106.   A PORT STOW: SHORTENING DOWN FOR FALMOUTH

107. NOW FOR SOME LETTERS!

108.  ROUND THE COAST TO THE CLYDE: PASSING THE CODLING LIGHT-SHIP

109.   THE LAST LANDMARK: PASSING AILSA CRAIG

110. MAKING THE SAILS FAST FOR THE LAST TIME

111.  "LEAVE HER, JOHNNIE, LEAVE HER!"  THE LOVELY LADY DESERTED IN
THE DOCKS

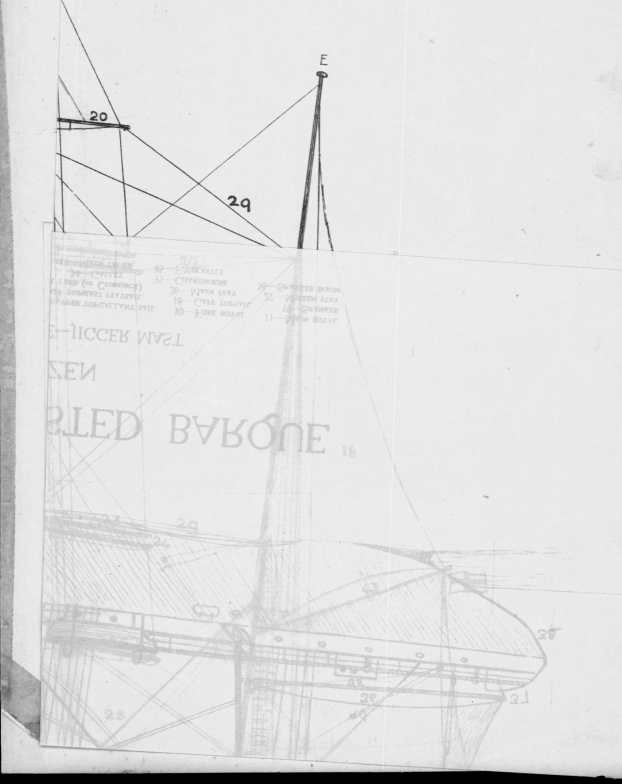